Graphic Organizers in Social Studies™

Learning About Urban Growth in America with Graphic Organizers

Linda Wirkner

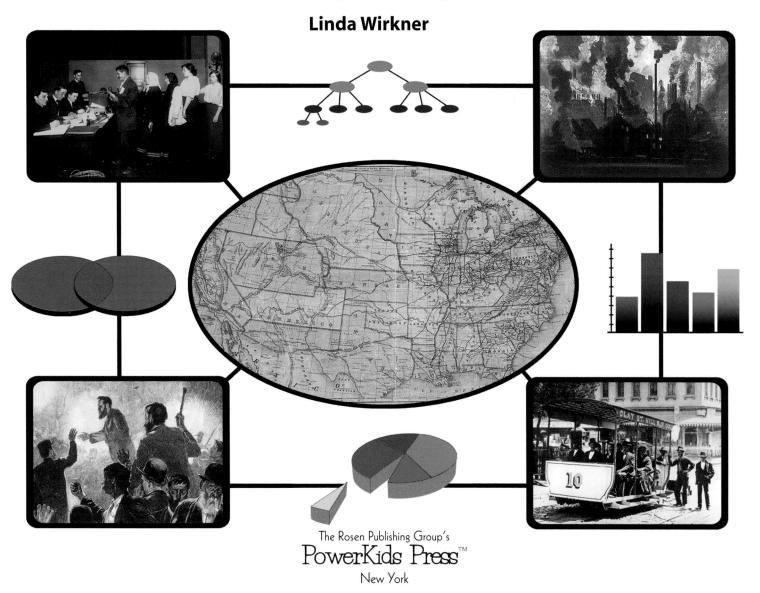

The Rosen Publishing Group's
PowerKids Press™
New York

To Ray, Pat, and Jo—super siblings

Published in 2005 by The Rosen Publishing Group, Inc.
29 East 21st Street, New York, NY 10010

First Edition

Editor: Orli Zuravicky
Book Design: Michael Caroleo

Photo Credits: Cover and title page (center) © Royalty-Free/Corbis; cover and title page (top left), (bottom right), pp. 4 (right), 8 (top left), (bottom left) © Bettman/Corbis; cover and title page (top right), (bottom left), pp. 7, 8 (bottom right), 11, 12 (right), 15, 16 (bottom), © Northwind Picture Archives, p. 8 (top right) © Hulton-Deutsch/Corbis.

Library of Congress Cataloging-in-Publication Data

Wirkner, Linda.
Learning about urban growth in America with graphic organizers / Linda Wirkner.
    v. cm. — (Graphic organizers in social studies)
Includes bibliographical references and index.
Contents: The changing face of America — The new American city — Technology shapes the city — Immigrant communities — Labor unions — New class system in America — Urban culture — Urban life changes rural life — The birth of the suburbs — Today's modern cities.
ISBN 1-4042-2809-8 (lib. bdg.) – ISBN 1-4042-5048-4 (pbk.)
1. Urbanization—United States—Juvenile literature. 2. Cities and towns—United States—Growth—Juvenile literature. 3. Graphic organizers—Juvenile literature. [1. Urbanization. 2. Cities and towns—Growth.] I. Title.

HT384.U5W57 2005
307.76'0973—dc22
                                        2003026927

Manufactured in the United States of America

Contents

Bar Graph: Three Waves of Immigration 1815–1914

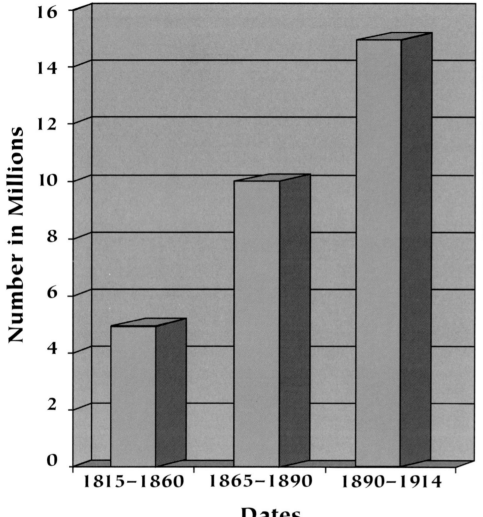

This photograph, taken between 1880 and 1910, shows immigrants lining up to have their immigration papers checked at Ellis Island, in New York City. Each immigrant had to go through many tests in order to be allowed into the country. Many immigrants were turned away because of sickness.

Number of Immigrants

Years	Number of Immigrants
1815–1860	5 million
1865–1890	10 million
1890–1914	15 million

The Changing Face of America

In the mid 1800s, American cities were fairly small. Homes and shops were grouped close together. Most people lived in the country. Only about 20 percent of the population lived in **urban** areas. By the late 1800s, better forms of **transportation** had come into use, making it much easier to travel from the country to the city. Steam-powered engines **spurred** the growth of factories. Factories opened in cities all over the Northeast, creating new jobs. People flocked to these cities to find work. **Immigrants** from Ireland, China, Poland, Russia, and other countries came to American cities hoping to find jobs and a better life. By 1910, more than 40 percent of the population lived in cities. The growth of American cities changed America forever. In this book you will learn about America's urban growth with graphic organizers. Graphic organizers are tools that help you to arrange facts.

A bar graph shows how different facts compare to each other. This bar graph shows how many immigrants came to America during each time period. Notice that the numbers are marked in millions. Around 30 million immigrants came between 1815 and 1914!

The New American City

Before the **Industrial Revolution**, cities were a mix of houses and small shops. Goods were handmade. After the Industrial Revolution, goods were made by machines. Machines produced more goods than people could make by hand. Products were made at lower costs, which meant they could be sold at cheaper prices. Small craft shops went out of business. Craftspeople moved from the country to cities to work in factories or stores. Tired of worrying whether their crops would be successful, farmers sold their farms and moved their families to cities.

Cities with factories became popular because they held the promise of jobs and higher salaries. However, they also filled American cities with noise and clouds of black smoke that came from the machines. Cities became dirty, crowded, and noisy. The slow-paced, quiet city became a thing of the past.

This graphic organizer is a compare/contrast chart. A compare/contrast chart is used to show what is alike and different between connected subjects. This chart shows what the manufacturing industry in America was like both before and after the Industrial Revolution.

Compare/Contrast Chart: Before and After the Industrial Revolution

	Before	After
Production of Goods	Goods were produced by skilled craftspeople. The production of goods took a long time and was often expensive.	Steam-powered machines mass-produced goods quickly and for less money than people could by hand.
Home-run Stores and Shops	The city was made up of a mix of houses and small craft shops.	The small craft shops disappeared because factories put them out of business.
Where People Lived	Most people lived in rural, or country, areas and little towns.	Most people lived in cities because they worked in factories.
Jobs	Most people were farmers or craftspeople. However, both types of jobs were uncertain. Farmers often lost their crops because of bad weather. Craftspeople were not always needed.	With the rise of factories came more job opportunities and higher salaries. Factory work was always certain, and workers did not have to be skilled to operate the machines.

This is a hand-colored image of the steel factories in Pittsburgh, Pennsylvania. During the nineteenth century, Pittsburgh became America's most industrialized city. It was called the "steel city" for its steel production, and the "smoky city" for the factory smoke that filled the air.

Concept Web: Mass Transit in the Late 1800s

CABLE CAR
The first cable car ran in San Francisco, California, in 1873. Cable cars were streetcars that were pulled by a long cable, which moved slowly under the city's streets. The cable car could go around corners and up and down hills. This was the first time that it was possible for streetcars to move without being pulled by horses.

ELEVATED RAILWAY
An elevated railway was a railroad on a big, long bridge, which was built over a city street. The first elevated railway was built in New York City, New York, and started running in 1871.

Mass Transit

TROLLEY
The first trolley was built in Richmond, Virginia, in 1888. Trolley cars were small electric trains. An electrical wire system was built over the streets. It was connected to a power station. The trolley was connected to the wire by a long pole. This gave the trolley electricity to use.

SUBWAY
America's first subway opened in Boston on September 1, 1897. It ran underground and used electricity to run its cars and trains. Subways were built as one answer to the problems that railways above the ground created, such as noise and fires from hot coals flying off the train. Subways were a huge success.

Technology Shapes the City

America's early buildings were made of brick, or a heavy clay, and stone. They were so heavy that buildings could be only a few stories high. In 1854, Elisha Graves Otis showed that his elevator with a brake could carry people safely. Builders began to include elevators in their buildings. By 1864, Sir Henry Bessemer's fast, inexpensive steelmaking method had come to America. Because steel was light and strong, people were able to build tall, narrow buildings known as skyscrapers. In 1883, New Yorker John Augustus Roebling completed the Brooklyn Bridge. It was the first **suspension bridge** to be held up by steel cables. As cities grew, it was no longer easy for people to walk to work. **Technology** made travel easier with **mass transit**. Buses, streetcars, **trolleys**, and subways, or underground trains, carried the growing city populations from place to place quickly.

This graphic organizer is a concept web. The main idea is written in the center of the web, while other connected ideas are written around it. This concept web is about mass transit in new American cities. The pictures show what each type of transit looked like.

Immigrant Communities

Between 1870 and 1900, more than 10 million immigrants came to America. Around 70 percent of them entered through the entrance called the Golden Door, located at Castle Garden, and later, Ellis Island, in New York City. Most immigrants settled in cities where jobs in meatpacking, steel, and iron industries were plentiful. Immigrants settled where people from their home country already lived. There they could cook their native foods and speak their own languages. Immigrant communities began as **slums**, since immigrants had little money. They shared small apartments with many families and took whatever jobs they could get. Many immigrants opened **ethnic** restaurants or food stores. Although America promised a better future, immigrant life was hard. These ethnic neighborhoods became a part of America's history. Some places, such as China Town and Little Italy, still exist today.

This is a cause-and-effect chart. An effect is an event or something that happens as a result of something else. A cause is something that makes an effect happen. This cause-and-effect chart shows how immigration changed American cities. The causes are on the left and the effects are on the right.

Cause-and-Effect Chart: Immigration in American Cities

Cause

Effect

Cause	Effect
Immigrants came in large groups to America and settled mostly in cities.	Cities became overcrowded, and so they expanded, or grew to take over more space.
Immigrants brought their culture and customs, or special practices, with them.	Ethnic communities were created and cities became populated with ethnic restaurants and stores.
Most immigrants were poor, so they took jobs in factories for little money.	Cheap immigrant labor allowed factories to produce a lot at a small cost.

This hand-colored image from the 1890s shows vendors, or salespeople, on Mulberry Street, in New York City. Mulberry Street was a popular place for Italian immigrants to settle. Mulberry Street is still the heart of Little Italy today, although the Italian population living there is only about 5,000. This number is much smaller than the 40,000 that lived there in the late 1800s.

11

Line Graph: Membership in Labor Unions 1900–1920

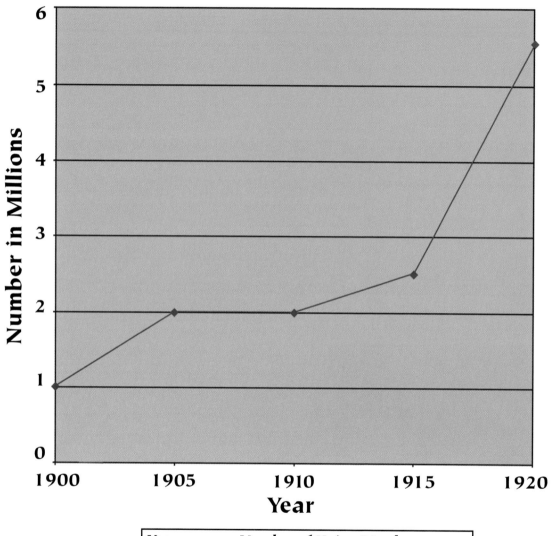

Number in Millions (y-axis: 0, 1, 2, 3, 4, 5, 6)

Year (x-axis: 1900, 1905, 1910, 1915, 1920)

Year	Number of Union Members
1900	1 million
1905	2 million
1910	2 million
1915	2.5 million
1920	5.5 million

This is a hand-colored image of the riot, or fight, that took place in Haymarket Square on May 4, 1886, in Chicago, Illinois. Four days before that, labor unions began a movement to limit the work day to eight hours. What began as a peaceful gathering became a terrible fight when a bomb went off in the crowd.

12

Labor Unions

To produce enough goods to make a **profit**, employers made laborers work from 70 to 80 hours per week. Wages were low and factories were dirty and unsafe. In the early 1900s, workers formed groups called labor unions to stand up to their **employers**. Union members asked for higher wages and shorter hours. When employers said no, workers went on strike, or refused to work.

At this time, it was also acceptable to employ children in factories and mines. Families were poor. They sent their children to work to make extra money. Working taught children **responsibility**. However, it also meant that children as young as five years old were operating **dangerous** machines. In 1916, Congress passed the first Child Labor Law. The law limited the ages at which children could begin to work and what type of work children could do.

This graphic organizer is a line graph. Line graphs can be used to show how something has changed over a period of time, or how two things compare to each other. This graph shows the growth in labor union membership from 1900 to 1920.

American Society

Along with industrial and urban growth came the rise of new upper, middle, and lower classes in American society. The upper class was made up of wealthy factory owners and industrialists. These people had made money in railroads, iron, steel, and **publishing**. The upper class enjoyed all of the good things cities offered, such as theater, music, art, and sports. They lived in big homes and dined in the finest restaurants. Store managers, clerks, and salespeople became America's middle class. They lived in nice houses or apartments. They could afford to enjoy many, but not all, of the advantages of city living. Life for the lower working class was quite different. Low wages made it a struggle for workers to put enough food on the table. They could only afford to live in tiny, uncomfortable apartments. Long hours laboring in factories left the lower class little time for pleasurable activities.

This graphic organizer is a classifying web. It organizes different groups of ideas and tells certain facts about each group. Facts are grouped together based on what they have in common. This web shows the three classes of American society and the differences in their lifestyles.

Classifying Web: American Society During the Industrial Revolution

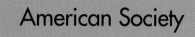

American Society

Upper Class

- Made up of wealthy factory owners and industrialists.
- They lived in the finest homes, ate the best food, and enjoyed all that the city offered.
- Some had money in railroads, iron, publishing, and steel.

Middle Class

- They lived in well-kept houses and apartments.
- They were able to enjoy some, but not all, of the good things that the city had to offer.
- Made up of small business managers, clerks, and salespeople.

Lower Class

- Made up of factory workers and unskilled laborers.
- They lived in tiny apartments that were too hot in the summer and too cold in the winter.
- They had no money or time to enjoy the city's activities. Their wages were so low that often they had to struggle to put food on the table.

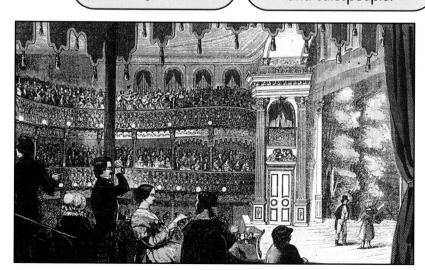

This hand-colored woodcut shows the Lecture Room at P. T. Barnum's American Museum. This room was used for all types of performances from theater to art shows. For 25 cents, people could enjoy all sorts of entertainment.

15

Map: Laws Passed Forcing Children to Attend School in the United States

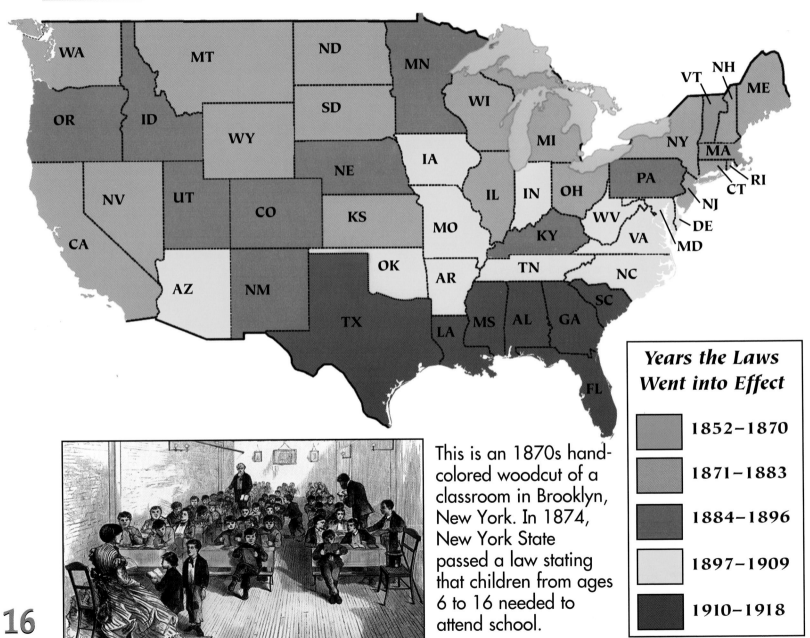

This is an 1870s hand-colored woodcut of a classroom in Brooklyn, New York. In 1874, New York State passed a law stating that children from ages 6 to 16 needed to attend school.

Years the Laws Went into Effect

- 1852–1870
- 1871–1883
- 1884–1896
- 1897–1909
- 1910–1918

Urban Life

Before the rise of the American city, **entertainment** occurred mostly at home. Towns were far apart from one another, and traveling was hard. The growth of urban mass transit made it possible for large numbers of people to travel to and from cities to attend concerts, plays, art displays, and sporting events. As labor unions succeeded in shortening the work day, people had more time to attend local events and to educate themselves on world events. They read newspapers such as the *New York Times*, the *Boston Globe*, and the *Washington Post*. Public school education grew in urban areas when city officials recognized the need for the children of immigrants to learn English. States began passing education laws that lengthened the school year and forced children to attend school. Between 1870 and 1900, school attendance increased by about eight million students.

This graphic organizer is a map. Maps can show where certain places are located or where and when certain events took place. This map of the United States shows in which time period each state passed school attendance laws. Be sure to look at the key to see what the colors stand for.

Changes in Country Life

In 1860, 80 percent of the nation's population still lived on farms or in small villages, and **agriculture** was a huge part of America's **economy**. The Industrial Revolution gave farmers new engine-powered farm machinery, which made their work faster and easier. Although many industries succeeded largely because of new technologies, the farming industry suffered from them. Using an engine-powered machine, one man could cut as much hay or wheat as four men could using older tools. Farmers were producing a **surplus** of crops so they had to charge less for the goods. Many farmers were forced out of farming because they were not able to make enough money to cover their expenses. Thousands of people went from being farmers to being workers in shops, mills, and factories. This upset in the farming industry changed Americans into a population of city-**dwellers**.

Pie charts show percentages, or parts of 100. Each slice of the pie stands for a different percentage. These charts show the change in urban and rural, or country, populations in 1860 and in 1910.

Pie Chart: America's Population

Year	Urban Population	Rural Population
1860	6,216,518	25,226,803
1910	42,064,001	50,164,495

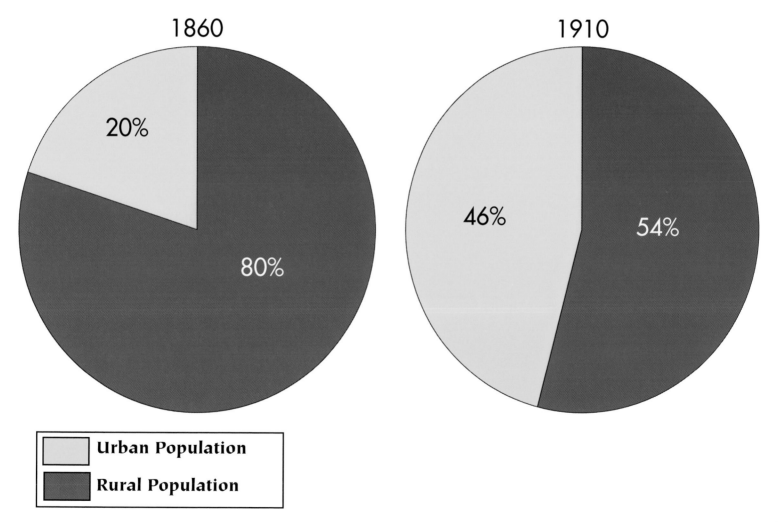

Timeline: Events That Led to America's Urban Growth

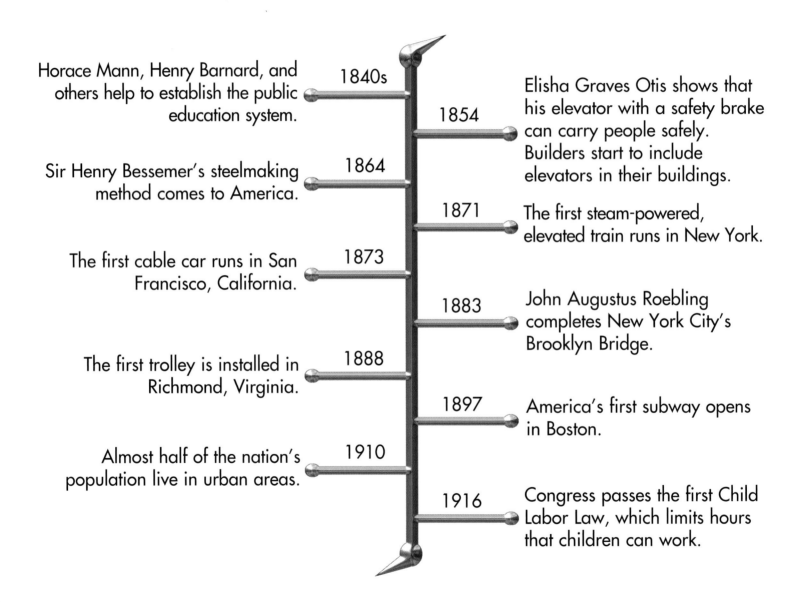

1840s — Horace Mann, Henry Barnard, and others help to establish the public education system.

1854 — Elisha Graves Otis shows that his elevator with a safety brake can carry people safely. Builders start to include elevators in their buildings.

1864 — Sir Henry Bessemer's steelmaking method comes to America.

1871 — The first steam-powered, elevated train runs in New York.

1873 — The first cable car runs in San Francisco, California.

1883 — John Augustus Roebling completes New York City's Brooklyn Bridge.

1888 — The first trolley is installed in Richmond, Virginia.

1897 — America's first subway opens in Boston.

1910 — Almost half of the nation's population live in urban areas.

1916 — Congress passes the first Child Labor Law, which limits hours that children can work.

The Birth of the Suburbs

As time went on, cities became too crowded. People did not want to live in small, dark city apartments any longer. Mass transit made it possible for people to live outside the city even though they worked inside the city. Those middle-class and upper-class families who could afford to leave the city wanted homes with big windows and backyards. The lack of housing in some crowded cities led builders to look beyond urban areas. They began to turn the farmlands located outside cities into housing **developments**. These developments became known as **suburbs**. Neighborhoods filled with small- and medium-sized homes took over fields and pastures. In the 1950s, William Levitt purchased a potato farm on Long Island, outside New York City, and built a community he called Levittown. Young couples could afford to buy their first home and moved happily to the suburbs.

This graphic organizer is a timeline. Timelines can help you study a period of history by listing important events that occurred during that time and what year they took place. This timeline lists some important events that led to the rise of the American city and urban growth.

Today's Modern Cities

Large cities all over the country became surrounded by ever-growing suburbs. In some parts of the country, these areas began to grow into one another, creating huge, super-city areas such as New York City, northern New Jersey, and Long Island. Over the years, as suburbs continued to grow, central city areas became rundown. People left cities to enjoy larger, nicer homes. The cheap city housing was left to lower-class families. In the early 1800s, the wealthy lived in the city centers and the poor lived outside the city. By the 1900s, it was quite the opposite. Today cities are home to people of all backgrounds and classes. City officials recognize the need for urban improvement in lower-class neighborhoods and work to better the conditions there. Many cities, such as New York City, have changed their rundown urban centers into successful business and **residential** communities. Cities continue to be the social centers of America.

Glossary

agriculture (A-grih-kul-cher) The science of producing crops and raising livestock, or animals.

dangerous (DAYN-jer-us) Able to cause harm.

developments (dih-VEH-lup-mints) Places where many houses are being built.

dwellers (DWEL-erz) Those who live in a certain place.

economy (ih-KAH-nuh-mee) The way in which a country or business manages its supplies and energy sources.

employers (im-PLOY-erz) People or businesses that hire one or more people for wages.

entertainment (en-ter-TAYN-ment) Something that brings pleasure or enjoyment.

ethnic (ETH-nik) Relating to a group of people who have the same race, nationality, beliefs, and ways of living.

immigrants (IH-muh-grints) People who move to a new country from another country.

Industrial Revolution (in-DUS-tree-ul reh-vuh-LOO-shun) A time in history beginning in the mid-1700s, when power-driven machines were first used to produce goods in large amounts.

mass transit (MAS TRAN-sit) A system of local public ways to travel in a city.

profit (PRAH-fit) The money a company makes after all its bills are paid.

publishing (PUH-blish-ing) The business of printing written documents.

residential (reh-zih-DEN-shul) Of or relating to where people live.

responsibility (rih-spon-sih-BIH-lih-tee) Something that a person must take care of or complete.

slums (SLUMZ) Rundown parts of a city that are often inhabited by poor people.

spurred (SPERD) Started or caused.

suburbs (SUH-berbz) Areas of homes and businesses that are near large cities.

surplus (SUR-plus) More than enough.

suspension bridge (suh-SPEN-shun BRIDJ) A bridge that hangs down from cables.

technology (tek-NAH-luh-jee) The way that people do something using tools.

transportation (tranz-per-TAY-shun) A way of traveling from one place to another.

trolleys (TRAH-leez) Streetcars.

urban (UR-ben) Having to do with a city.

Index

Web Sites

Due to the changing nature of Internet links, PowerKids Press has developed an online list of Web sites related to the subject of this book. This site is updated regularly. Please use this link to access the list:
www.powerkidslinks.com/goss/urbango/